History in Living Memory

Entertainment Through the Years

How Having Fun Has Changed in Living Memory

Clare Lewis

heinemann
raintree

To contact Capstone Global Library please
call 800-747-4992, or visit our web site
www.capstonepub.com

Edited by Clare Lewis and Holly Beaumont
Designed by Philippa Jenkins
Picture research by Tracy Cummins
Production by Victoria Fitzgerald
Originated by Capstone Global Library Ltd
Printed and bound in China by Leo Paper Group

18 17 16 15 14
10 9 8 7 6 5 4 3 2 1

Library of Congress Cataloging-in-Publication Data
Lewis, Clare, 1976-
   Entertainment through the years : how having fun has changed in living memory / Clare Lewis.
      pages cm.—(History in living memory)
   Includes bibliographical references and index.
   ISBN 978-1-4846-0923-1 (hb)—ISBN 978-1-4846-0928-6 (pb)—ISBN 978-1-4846-0938-5 (ebook) 1. Popular culture—Juvenile literature. 2. Amusements—Juvenile literature. 3. Mass media—Juvenile literature. I. Title.

HM621.L485 2015
306—dc23   2014015027

This book has been officially leveled by using the F&P Text Level Gradient™ Leveling System.

Acknowledgments
We would like to thank the following for permission to reproduce photographs: Capstone Press: Philippa Jenkins, 1 Bottom Right, 1 Top Left; Corbis: ©D&P Valenti/ClassicStock, 17; Corel: 4; Flickr: John Atherton, Cover Top; Getty Images: David Hanover, 19, Gamma-Keystone, 12, Imagno, 15, L. Willinger/FPG/Hulton Archive, 14, Richi Howell/Redferns, 9; Shutterstock: aopsan, 23 Top, AVAVA, Cover Bottom, Dan Kosmayer, 23 Middle, Diego Cervo, 20, Flas100, Design Element, Panom Pensawang, 22 Top Right, racorn, 22 Bottom, Samuel Borges Photography, 21, Studio DMM Photography, Designs & Art, Design Element, Vector Department, 23 Bottom, ZanyZeus, 22 Top Left; SuperStock: ClassicStock.com, 5, 8, 10, Cusp, 16, Marka, 6, Superstock, 7, Transtock, 11, 13; Thinkstock: Creatas, 18, Back Cover.

Every effort has been made to contact copyright holders of material reproduced in this book. Any omissions will be rectified in subsequent printings if notice is given to the publisher.

Some words are shown in bold, **like this**. You can find them in the glossary on page 23.

Contents

What Is History in Living Memory?

Some history happened a very long time ago. Nobody alive now lived through it.

Some history did not happen very long ago. Our parents, grandparents, and adult friends can tell us how life used to be. We call this history in living memory.

How Has Entertainment Changed in Living Memory?

The way people have fun has changed a lot since your grandparents were young. In the 1950s, there were no cell phones or computers.

Children listened to programs on the radio. They watched black-and-white movies at movie theaters.

How Did People Listen to Music in the 1950s?

People listened to music on the radio or on **record** players. In the 1950s, a new type of music called rock and roll became popular.

People loved to dance to rock-and-roll music. Teenagers gathered around record stores to hear the new songs.

How Did People Have Fun in the 1960s?

In the 1960s, more people had televisions. Television programs were now in color.

Like today, going to a movie theater was a fun treat. *Mary Poppins* was a popular movie in the 1960s.

How Did Your Parents and Grandparents Play?

In the olden days, there were fewer cars. Children played outside more than they do now.

Children climbed trees, skipped, and played baseball. Children still do these things today.

How Did Children Have Fun in the 1970s?

In the 1970s, Barbie dolls were a popular toy. Children also played board games, **marbles**, and hide-and-seek.

Just like today, people enjoyed trips out with their family to museums. Museums weren't as hands-on as they are today.

What Changes Happened in the 1980s?

In the 1980s, **cassettes** began to be used to store and play music. Portable cassette players allowed people to listen to music while moving around outside.

Some people had computers at home for playing games. It could take 30 minutes for a game to load in those days!

How Did People Have Fun in the 1990s?

In the 1990s, most people listened to music on CDs. Video game consoles became very popular and easier to use.

The Internet became popular in the late 1990s. This made it easier for people from all over the world to talk together, play games together, and share ideas.

How Do You Have Fun Today?

Some things haven't changed in living memory. We still like to read books and play outside with our friends.

Some things have changed a lot. How do you play games and listen to music now?

Picture Quiz

Which of these could be played in the 1970s?

marbles

tablet games

video game console

How is this game different from many games you play today?

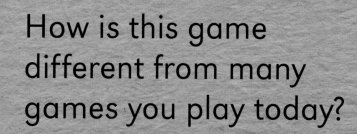

Answer: Marbles. You can play marbles without electricity or being connected to a computer.

Picture Glossary

cassette
small case with coiled tape inside. It was used for recording and playing music in the 1970s and 1980s.

marbles
colored glass balls used for playing games

record
round, flat piece of plastic. It was used for recording and playing music in the 1960s and 1970s.

Find Out More

Books

Hunter, Nick. *Talking About the Past* (History at Home). Chicago: Heinemann Library, 2014.

Rau, Dana Meachen. *Toys, Games, and Fun in American History*. Milwaukee: Weekly Reader Early Learning Library, 2007.

Web site

FactHound offers a safe, fun way to find Internet sites related to this book. All of the sites on FactHound have been researched by our staff.

Here's all you do: Visit www.facthound.com
Type in this code: 9781484609231

Index